THE TILT TORN AWAY FROM THE SEASONS

THE TILT TORN AWAY FROM THE SEASONS

POEMS

ELIZABETH LINDSEY ROGERS

ACRE

CINCINNATI 2020

Acre Books is made possible by the support of the Robert and Adele Schiff Foundation and the Department of English at the University of Cincinnati.

ISBN-10 (pbk) 1-946724-26-2 | ISBN-13 (pbk) 978-1-946724-26-7
ISBN-10 (ebook) 1-946724-27-0 | ISBN-13 (ebook) 978-1-946724-27-4

Designed by Barbara Neely Bourgoyne
Cover art: Mars Orbiter Laser Altimeter (MOLA) topographical map of Mars (detail), cylindrical projection, NASA.

The press is based at the University of Cincinnati, Department of English and Comparative Literature, McMicken Hall, Room 248, PO Box 210069, Cincinnati, OH, 45221–0069.

Acre Books books may be purchased at a discount for educational use. For information please email business@acre-books.com.

This book is for my mother,

Lindsey T. Rogers.

Whoever deciphers these canyon walls
remains forsaken, alone with history,

no harbor for his dream.

—AGHA SHAHID ALI,
"I See Chile in My Rearview Mirror"

CONTENTS

THE FRONTIER

in many voices

THE FRONTIER

after the first 360-degree panoramic photograph of Mars

And all those years, we'd pictured fire—
a neon sign blinking
VACANCY—a world as red as that

inside our bodies, but without
the claustrophobia,
the low ceilings of our skin.

We didn't think of a sky
azure only at sunset,
or stones, a similar blue, scattered across the regolith.

Now, we know
this pair of weary moons:
the first one painfully slow, a pinprick

taking three days
to move across our vision.
The second, Phobos, is the western origin of fear.

Misshapen, mold-gray.
Every four hours, it rises
like the last potato of the famine.

And by now I know, as you must,
what it means to lose
your lakes and oceans. To creak inside

                                  the riverbed, cross its sockets

                    and arthritic elbows.

    To think of rain as a form, a tome

                           of bygone remedies.

               I can only dream

     of what snow must do for the desert.

                       The camera pans this world:

               Like earth, pocked

by canyons. Like Liberty, the surface looks aged,

                        a green patina.

             Over dune and dust, the Rover's

      tracks are the only disturbance.

                    Like a sidewinder, or wagon ruts

        the trail circles, and circles itself again.

   Again, the ground made

                  target practice. We come in peace

       Curiosity says. But that's how

    all our ships began.

                    As I land, I weigh next to

           nothing. I leap

three times as high. But there is no canopy,

no timber for an ax.
Apple seeds float. There won't be saplings
next year, though spring goes twice as long.

Imagine a Western
set, a terrain of glare and scour.
The unspoken agoraphobia

drives us all
into the saloon:
the sheriff, the unshaven rogue, the virgin

in blue gingham, the Indian,
and the hourglass whore.
Horses are dead. Whiskey's still

brown, but a grit in our throats.
The first shot sounds—
in air this thin, muted
as a powder puff.

On cue, we turn. Picture:
how slowly
the shutter swings, doors float open.

RED PLANET APPLICATION

When did you first become interested in space?

As a baby inside
bathwater, soap skidding

across the surface. The prisms
burst, their remnants

taking the form of oil.
As a teenager, I lit a match

in hydrogen's mouth
and listened for the pop.

What skills or qualities do you have that may aid the colony?

I am naturally calibrated
in zeros and ones. I was born

with this base-2 ability.
I can spot your wedding ring

no matter how lost
it is in a yard.

I also read bass clef.
I play the cello.

What experiences do you have with cultures other than your own?

Despite popular belief, I don't believe
China's Great Wall is visible from space.

I have shared bunks with many strangers.
Cotton ceilings shift above me.

Any allergies? Intolerances to heat, altitude, or cold?

In the desert, we call the sky
a star rash. We say we can sustain

our bodies entirely on rock
sugars and rock salts.

—A family history of cancer or osteoporosis?

A river underground,
I hear my marrow humming.

Have you ever been hospitalized for a psychological condition?

Now and then, there is a gray day
in the canyon. Walls know no noise.

Sometimes you do sense molecules
zinging past your eardrums.

You will never see your family or friends again. Discuss.

The brush of another person
is more gravity than I can stand.

Like a lantern's metal and paper
if you touch me, I may collapse. I have

sworn off skin to skin,
and not just during Lent.

Inside a bubble, I prefer to drift
at an arm's length.

Would you be willing to participate in a strenuous seven-year training program?

Someone smashed my rearview mirror.
It never meant that much to me.

If given four hundred feet of wire fencing—to enclose a sheep or goat pasture where grass is struggling—choose the shape that provides the maximum area.

8   O   ✓□   ◎

Which of the following is most unlike the others?

o   0**?**   ◯   ◎

Please retype this message (to prove you are not a robot):

: (t o b o r a t o n e r a u o y e v o r p o t) g n I w o l l o f e h t e p y t e r e s a e l P

And which of the following most resembles your self-portrait? You may only choose one.

A   ⌠   人   ✓⇑

DEEP SPACE CROWN

Out of the oval, we read darkness. Stars

glint like lost sequins or scales

numbering a knife's black edge.

Libra tips, its precarious justice

just beyond our reach.

This outer world wafts a summer: hot metal, diesel,

barbeque. But the moon, matte as wax paper,

smells more like gunpowder than egg or bread.

We flip through white-ink novels

typed on endless—negative—space, our bodies

diminished or augmented, never quite to actual scale.

This is how a meter grows

into a mile. The mile spins itself into a stone,

whooshing out and on and on.

Whooshing on and on, our bodies

are live cultures trapped

in this white capsule. We name ourselves

after flora, epiphytes drifting

in a realm of cold gas. What we sweat

or breathe out will circle, eventually,

back into the drinking glass.

Any ship is a hermetic

world: an arrow tightened,

blunt head swallowing the nock.

So forget that blue-and-cloud earth

fading in the porthole. Whatever roots

we have will dissolve. Mostly air and dust,

we wheel within a wheel. A body sure gets around.

Within the ship's sure body, a star wheel

replaces the wall calendar:

time's squares redrawn

with spidery legs, framed in concentric circles.

I hear the ratchet click, the only real noise

between the worlds' terrible blanks.

Tucked in my hollow space suit, I wanted

to be a rivet: my head brassy

and fixed, the analog in chaos.

But every human body

is a disaster, the fallout from old stars.

My brain is just a tangle of wire,

electricity clusters. My hair is recessive

rubble, all redshift and helium.

Imagine the sun as a red balloon, helium

colliding at its core. There, they say

a human's mongrel of atoms

will weigh twenty-eight times more.

I would never trust any hand of god

over gravity's colossal pull. How heavy

our limbs grow when faced with that

stove eye coming closer and closer.

Plasma smells like burning sugar.

On Earth, you dream of appliances

you forgot to turn off, children you abandoned,

and, if you're lucky, the power to fly.

In space, you dream only of feet

touching down on warm sand or wood.

Just sand and warm stone: the universe

is a Zen garden, or her third cousin

once removed. Mechanical arms

rake the surface, meditating on grooves

and swirls. Occasionally, we hallucinate

water inside a gravel's white spill.

Like the theater, space can render us

stiller than rock. When we do move, it is behind layers,

white scrim over cloak over skin. These costumes

keep us away from radiation,

the hot and cold knobs of other worlds.

What I would give now for a beach, the sand

white or red or basalt. My feet want

a real lip of water, not just a backdrop of blue.

Long ago, against a blue water backdrop,

we turned and turned, and mostly felt

nothing. We held ourselves up like trees

without wind. Whatever substance our spoon held

flowed straight from silver and into our mouths.

But now is not then.   Now is not even

now. Clock hands, craving sleep,

sloth toward the next white number.

       To think I once imagined space

as the smooth texture of coins

or zeros, and never as that deep sap

that traps and always keeps. Never

as our own atoms, suspended in this colloid:

inside the dark, these stars we circle and misread.

BACKFLASH: THE POOL AT THE PROSPEROUS HOTEL

Landlocked, nothing but dust
    on the winter route that brings us—the three-wheeled *bungbung*
                kicking up refuse from the road—past the smokestacks
      and dark pilings of the countryside. This, the nation's
iron and coal heart.

      We strip down to nothing. Slither
             into suits from another era:
        unnatural pinks and oranges,
a sunset's chemical warning.

      The shower room we lose
           inside a curfew of fog. Where I ask out loud
    厕所在那儿?
Where is the toilet?
        She motions at white grates
           X-ing the floor. To where a woman hovers.

        Down the tiled hallway: the basement's
chlorine light. A pair of plastic turrets
      half sunk in the blue center.
          No standard Soviet rectangle. Instead, a kidney.
    No lifeguard. Where are the children?

Twin slides spiral down
    like DNA, undone.
        Red ribbons—the color of good luck—

tie up their two closed entrances.
I remember children I passed
in town, their red limbs ending

at the elbow. The baby with six fingers.
And the man collecting trash
who lost his face in a chemical burn.
Someone help, I overheard. *I have to dig the wells deeper every year.*

Ankle, calf, knee—we lower ourselves into what
seems more algae, less chlorine.
There's a second just before
we give our limbs
to buoyancy. We flail a bit
in bluegreen. Our bodies are no lilies.

潜水吧, she urges.
Dive. My ears fill
with leaking sounds. In the cloudiness between,
I see her ponytail fan away.

I dreamed of water last night.
A river lined with rocks. So shallow
you could ford it, and your shins would still be dry.
But the surface was too shiny, stuck
to me like cellophane.
And then I saw the colliery's fortress,
a tank blocking the horizon.

What is it worth? I ask, looking down
through sludge. She pulls me
                                toward the castle underpass.
                                                You can't know, she says.
                                        When I was a child, we had nothing.

Light and heat
                fade out. A smell like bleach and spoiled vegetables.
                                                Is this a past? A future?
                                Our limbs tossing up
                crude bubbles, we round
                                this half-moon passage
                                                and hurry toward the ceiling, its weak fluorescent sun.

CUMBERLAND CITY, MARS

Our origin myth: one silver
arm, the robot boring
the first hole in rock—
what overturned

a powder, green as old coins
or the Statue of Liberty.
Here, a woman rose, created
in the mountains' image.

Ground, when tested, revealed
its alkalinity. We commenced a victory
garden of turnips and asparagus.
It's true. That wasn't enough.

So for a half mile
that arm kept digging, hungry
for loam or long-lost
honey or water in the rock,

but found the old veins,
star-crossed minerals, a mouth.
A clay world that buried itself alive—
in hopes it couldn't be claimed?

The man, when he landed, renamed
every place. This city he named for the gap.
For Kentucky Daniel, whose company
blazed through some wilderness.

Land was a throwaway word, the opposite
of water. It meant domain and the right
to mine, drillheads spinning
toward the core ~~of Earth~~.

Because he first assumed
a clean slate underneath us,
we filled that valley fast
with machines' carbon hiss

and our earpieces all droning
with the same hunting ballad.
Pitches slipped, the lines distorted
in the unstable, buffering air—

O sound the kill horn

across the face rocky rocky

O light out to the wild west

we need more elbow room—

like the first world, all new names
spring from nostalgia,
recall *X*'s on the emigration map
and erased trails of salt.

AMAZONIS, MARS

. . . what do you miss?
   Leaves, when they rustle,
a forest sounding like a forest

of paper dolls'
   green limbs. This I gave
up for the thrill

rising out of treeless
   colonies: a story of lava, free flow,
lacquering these next Great Plains.

There's one scar
   a river carved, but this ground isn't
a bible you know. True,

there are chapters
   of basalt and clay,
but no leaves get saved between them.

   The stone here shears itself. Minerals
glare so profusely, a broken plate
   comes to mind. How many

   have we dropped
on cell floors, hour after hour,
   not out of anger but sheer loneliness

   for a sense of time? Or sound?
The new world is mute
   to anything that lies inside

the human register. A yell
in my mother tongue
the thin air tries to flatten

into a snore.
And this plate my big hand spins
cannot whir, only mimics

our slow orbit, its muffle, dead
ice. Where I walk, my boot treads
cancel their own noise.

ASTROBLEME

Victoria Crater

Witch hazel I boil

below the silver rim,

my moonroof dark, beading sweat

like a horse's flank, from myth.

So what if Genghis Khan

worshipped nothing

but the sky?

I revere my own dark matter,

not just spittles of gas or light.

At dawn I chart my mood

across an analog screen,

sine wave hissing: a grass snake's

S, neon green.

The desert—embered, hormonal—

takes its first inhale. The sun

rises mad, a cigarette's end
poised above the canyon.

*

But all *sols* are the same. The grunt all morning,
rover wheels, friction
crossing the potholes. Damn this world!

Its forever adolescence,
face full of deep depressions, wounds.
Where terra once resigned itself—

laid its ugliness bare—
waxy grass, like Easter baskets',
now sprigs up through the crater.

*

In truth, I'm not much for fresh
beginnings. My skin feels fragile,
a blown green glass. I believe

a body's odor is better
than chemical cures, weapons
designed to wipe out the face.

So I live in fear of the next
bombardment, more waves
passing through the ground:

shatter cones and broken bowls
and my stone door rolling away.

*

No female can avoid
the Easter morning mandates:
bathe twice in something man-made,

waterless. Blot the blemish
with sterile hemp.
Apply the mineral mask, mica

colonizing us with that chaos
usually reserved for stars.

Unfold the pastel dress:

another cold year passed. (How

many hours, with radiation and wind,

before this lace

unravels back to its brides?)

The acolyte girls circle

around the escarpment,

our skins reflecting

that uncertain light—

So beautiful! So alive! the crowd exclaims.

We flare. They call it spring.

BACKFLASH: HINGE

If I could turn
      back—not girlhood, but before—
            I'd be an oyster's

spit-sheen, drift first as a spat.
          Smaller than a pinkie
               nail polished

for junior prom. I'd pick
        my own debut,
            starting here, at the hinge.

In saline, where the first
         attachments form, but before
               the complications

of buckling
      down in bed. Before calcium
            spit into rings

of protection, before the need
         to count back to the rock.
               I'd choose blood

without color, pre-
        scarlet drawn by needles.
              I won't be marked
O or *X*. I settle now
        for water, the easy
           plain of cells.

The gray sea umbrella
            lets some light
                        in, refuses the rest. Below
we know to filter
            slime, slung mud,
                        to quarantine—

myth or not—our irritants with nacre.
                        Before the snare
                                    of sex—*Cross your legs*

or *It's not personal*—I'll learn a self-
                        reliance. I'll fashion

two hard lips
            to house my feeler
                        and lacy mantle.

Landing, we block out
            euphemism: no "naughty pearl,"

"no-no button," or
            "little man in a boat."
                        There's not a language

where we latch. Just laissez-faire
            anatomy, and watered sounds
                        we don't decode.

LOLITA'S ROVER BALLAD

So this dune buggy trip
leaves me all rotten
inside. I'm sick of learning
landforms: dried-up lake beds,

sore in their salts, all my wants
under haze and burned-up rubber.
Between winks of sleep, I see
canyons in split pastels

(my half-eaten jawbreakers),
pink clouds drifting above, bored
as a flock of sheep. I've re-counted
my bottle caps, pressed my lips

to glossy magazines. I taught myself
how to peel bananas with my feet.
So what? It's a free country. I think.
But all time is stuck. I'm twelve

now and forever. I turn and turn and turn
but there's nowhere else to go.

Oh wow. More desert. "Motels"
crop up like mushrooms,
then poof. Long-legged,
neon signs erase themselves

behind the ugly dust devils.
Dress me up as another Dorothy,
braids, I guess, and dirty blue
gingham. Trade my **** again

for something made of candy.
A frontier ought to be exciting
things: cities made of windows,
secret red rock caves. Right now

I want more records. To get
myself a dog. Own a hothouse
where the sugarcane sways
like a bunch of girls dancing to the radio.

BACKFLASH: GIRL MYTH

And while her right hand
  cradled the old blue telephone,
the left snaked
  around my ribs

like those bracings
  between cliff and vista,
or a parent holding
  a child up to see

the parade. This is how
  she would lead me
out into the green
  ardor, those subtropical woods

in May. See it clearly
  now: a girl walks, bold,
following—no god,
  but this woman

until the girl's corralled
  by trees, swallowed inside
their silent ring.
   As it was for Daphne, new leaves

unfisted with such fury,
  I could have never counted
them all. But when she
  first lifted her hand

to my ear, I felt
  the end and beginning
of each nerve, that live web
  under the skin: shimmer,

dew, sparks. What is it
        I asked, but already
she was riding the glissando
        down and down,

pausing only to consider
        knots, those two
pinks—like her own—
        rising above my ribs.
                When that first word, love,

slipped out of my mouth,
        it was like a strange bird
the wrong wind
        gets hold of,

an orange bird hurricaned
        into the deciduous world,
then held against the dead
        weight of wood. Oh, I

was far from home.
        I should've called
my mother but forgot her
        while the slate-colored clouds

began to part. The tallest tree
        dressed itself in a sash,
a light sifting somewhere
        between brainwash

and complete tenderness.
      There is always this
denial, scandering along
        any form of knowledge:

she, who will always say
        No, no, it never happened
like that, that way
        you are telling it. How am I

left, then, to explain
        my body's deep whorl,
the permanent arches etched
        into me. By who else's hand?

What chronology cannot
      be counted by rings.
It is impossible. She wants
      to convince me

of how every girl gives
      birth to herself: her hands
clutching the troubled cord,
      one foot snared along its root.

ECOPOIESIS

The Terraforming

(PHASE I)

                            They said we could bring nothing with us.
                 That we would fashion a new
world, start from the lichens up.

                       That algae had begun its alien, rash-like blooming.
            Mirrors had turned the planet
from death to death warmed over.

                         Over time, we would adjust
               to the usual frontier
smells—iron and blood, their tang

                          almost the same—
         and the native winds, so unbridled,
carrying the sweet stench of sagebrush.

                         Then, the playas' cold saline.
         And soft traps, floral vapors
where permafrost had started to give.

(PHASE II)

                                        To enter the iron lungs
                    of space and time, you must prove
your mint condition. Your heart cannot be

                                        weak or damaged.
                    Valves must slide easily:
    in space, there is no room for struggle.

                                        Breathing requires violence:
                    the red planet's hyle
split back to the atom. They call oxygen

                                        invisible. But dust-free is
                    so rare in this world
            that clarity is a lavish color.

(PHASE III)

We've tunneled under karst, settled
on treeless avenues.
Our addresses numbered in the old
Roman way. Our subdivided homes
carved along ancient
ruts, the lava tubes.

The whole cruel spring, the dust-storm
(inverse-monsoon) season, we've kept
ourselves underground. We call this life
in the manhole.
But what is runoff?
What is a man?

(PHASE IV)

I think back to my last night on Earth.
It was winter, just after Christmas.
I couldn't stop staring

at the threadbare trees:
like nerve endings, backlit on night's fovea.
And in morning, when blue

broke through, the trees were like ink veins
on a swatch of skin or parchment.

I can't say what I felt
on my final look: the salt-swirled
Earth, its impossible cobalt. But when

my eye caught its last curve,
the arc of gravitas & history,
I hope, also began to dissolve.

(PHASE V)

This time, we'll form more carefully.

We've started on empty

plains. We'll vaccinate. We'll make the new deal fair.

Until rain is reliable, we'll modify

our grain indoors.

They say in meteor basins, cheatgrass will

proliferate. And if the place is

both barren and virgin, there's no such thing

as an invasive species.

When the dust clears, we go out.
A figure interrupts the horizon. She tests
her weight against rocks and moss's scattered pixels.

She has heard only
of the old world, what was swallowed
by heat and storm and saltwater.

What can I tell her. Who doesn't crave
their own expansion,
breathing in this open space:

*I would not exchange my home
on the range for all of the cities so bright.*
The red man [sic] *was pressed*

from this part of the West.
He's likely no more to return. Oh,

I take my empty cup
to a next-door neighbor.
She jokes: We're a leg's length away

from an equator. Can't we have
someone grow us more sugar?

(PHASE VII)

But I see, from behind

glass, the curfew

of my helmet: the bulge of Tharsis,

three inert mountains, now patched in green,

and lightning-rod spires, pricking

the thin somewhere just beyond.

Beyond that, night's three brightest figures:

two moons, named in Greek

for *dread* and *fear.*

And below them,

Earth? A flickering, lost blue pilot:

*

I wonder   as I wander

out under the sky . . .

ARCADIA, MARS

To console myself, I wander
wing to wing in the orangery,
        slip between twisted limbs,
olives' silver and green. The air here
        whisks so convincingly I can't believe
 there's a rock partition keeping me
        safe from the pinked-out sky.

In Gethsemane—that ancient other world—
        they say the Virgin Mary
is also buried in a silver grove.
        They say any rock is agony. They say her grief
was deeper than those roots
        (the oldest known on Earth).

Our own carbon dates us. If I could cut
        myself open, you'd see rings
lapping more rings: my mother
        crying for her mother in the same
way her mother wept for hers.
        You'd see the silvery orbit

where each life dissolved.
        But for now, I remain
human. I am a nesting doll for griefs.
        Even in utopia, there is suffering:
one sheep forced to walk
        the labyrinth, ensuring the grass
regenerates. And my young daughter,
        her legs thin as reeds,

chased and caught and pushed by
        the boys again. Her layers stripped away.

Not even the olive he wedged
       under her tongue
could hold her, clot those cries—
       these shepherds, they think of nothing but
what might wake this weak blue soil.

BLUELESS BAY

in many voices

EARTH, TORN AND TURNED

        The night, uranium orange,
keeps its fever close to the horizon.
All waves of grain

we gnaw to brooms,
bristles rasping at sky.

I skid on embers
to the watering hole, searching for what

resembles a family face.   Whoever's left
will learn the meaning

of opaque. Nothing
here but clots

of algae. The last of it
floats where the mirror did, in myth.

Whoever spoke of love
      among the ruins

saw the world through
a pinhole, an index card

      punched for eclipse. They did not flee
the shore, gripping
the last of the picnic's plastic

straws. Or worry much
about the earth or how

much of it is covered
by water, or salts.

Somewhere north
you cannot point to, now that the graph
                    has shifted—the slack net

thrown off, the water
muddy, uncharted—

a handful of turbines
have tumbled off their rig,
                    the rotors floating

like petals in oil, or bodies
inside a dead sea.

How could we have known
the decade begins this way:
            tensile-strength carbon, what snaps

more easily than saltines.
            There are no birds on the sea.

Only white blades float.
These spinning machines—first in Sistan, Alexandria,

and now here, placed
as an afterthought—we built

with the best of intentions. We meant them

to outlast us, stand
in for our misgivings. And to colonize,

        far from land, the last of
the old world's scattered wind.

COLUMBUS, MARS

Just when we agreed
we'd overreached, touched
that ragged, final edge,
the next continent began
drifting toward us, floe
shushing its own pink name.

At first, dreamed up—
a soap bubble's
laminous prism—

then, the separate colors
clicking into focus.
Then, embers. Shore of ash.

Like the old world's
temperas, it darkened
the longer we threw our light upon it,

though we still claimed
each crater rim,
what beveled just below

the surface. Each had its memory
of water, rust like a bathtub's ring.
Red sky at night,

sailor's delight. . . .
    We were half-drunk when
        we landed, cruel on our own iron taste.

Out of thin air, we became
    toponymists, touched every place
        we'd named:

alluring   *transfixed*

    fertile?   *inclined to love*

        Who would stop us

from drawing this map too,
    in a girl's naked image?

Hail the *Santa Maria*, full
    of plastic grace. We bottled
        and vialed minerals, new flora,

scrawled our stories
    on her cabin walls—
        in white ink, a mythic code—

tell the kids:
    Long ago, a fleet of men
        let their parachutes bloom

over desiccated ground.
The lost blue pilot felt
the wind tear at his face

just before his feet touched down,
his mind gone blank, like sailcloth.

BACKFLASH: SEVEN CATASTROPHES

ORIGIN

The guide knifes an imaginary slit
from breastbone down to the navel,
then branches into two at her legs, hung off
the execution stone. *This is how they did it*, he says,
*to criminals in ancient times. We are all Christians
now.* They give us tours, beer, and barbeque.
A Batak house is shaped like an ark:
on stilts to keep out water and to hold
the pigs and buffalo below. At night,
their lowing shakes the kitchen floor.
Leave us alone, they are saying. Bodies—
of animals, or water—never ask to be held.
Men sleep alone, against the front gable. The roof
rises at both ends: stern and bow, or pair of horns.

MINERAL

Rising over the hill, we count pairs of horns
against a green so profuse it might damage
the eye. When I close mine, color
still flashes, neon like betta fish
darting through the flooded paddies.
Who am I to see this place? Saturation is a blue
crater, a lake reflecting the heavy sky,
and the cotton sarongs we hung up days ago
that still haven't dried on the line.

When I climb and slip, a bruise spreads
on my hip like a caldera: cold basalt
at the center, silica at the shallow edge.
When I move, it shimmers into living: a moth
scratching the lamp, too hot where we try to touch.

ASH

Hot is the itch we know
when spinning a yarn
about the earth's ejecta, but after
the volcano, weren't there years
without summer? This continent
swathed in six inches of gray?
Pyroclasts veiled the planet, kept it away
from the rain and sun. Wilt flattened
the forest, concaved the human belly.
And always that sound of small gods
that could be carried on wind.
The population P whittled
to a waiflike $\int$ the ship slid
in the bottleneck, and through.

CURRENCY

Because the bottleneck theory
tells us that a ship can flatten
a nation, one ship always leads

to another and then its company
digging up the land. When ripe
coffee beans bulge—red as lungs'
alveoli—some drop and spoil before
they're plucked, the fields a small massacre.
The remaining cherries must be
scoured and rinsed and what now
do we do with gallons of wastewater.
Pour it back in the lake? Dumb down
its original clarity? Dead fish float
to the top, rafts with their silver sides up.

LOOKOUT

They promised rice, a sunny-side up,
and kopi in glass tumblers. But they never said the inn
was clapboard and shambles. The island's pinnacle
is a wrecked crow's nest, far from the harbor's pizza,
English marquees: WE TOP WITH MAGIC MUSHROOMS.
Crows sway in these tropical pines. The women chew
their betel, smiles as orange as iodine.
The young one ushers us to where we sleep:
a barn with a bed touching all four walls.
But I climb out at night, urgent
and shivering, leap over the snouts
of three sleeping dogs. To pee in the dark
I hover, lift my hem over the soil,
as I've seen the other women do in daylight.

FLESH

What Marco Polo saw he never recorded in daylight,
preferring chicken-scratch in the dark, his feather pen's
white the only light to see by. *These hill folk are man-eaters.*
They suck out human bones. Kin must provide pepper, lemons, and salt.
He saw this, somehow, all the way from the coast, having never
left the beach's hem, pressed into the Batak interior.
These women, he wrote, *in truth, are very handsome, very sensual.*
I remember Elizabeth Taylor on a Spanish beach,
nipples boring through her white bathing suit. The boys
flock and circle her because she doesn't belong.
And way back in time, under rings of candlelight,
Columbus is footnoting Polo's *Travels*,
the pages oily with his touch. The ink splashes
beneath his hand: a mix of acid, salts, and gall.

SHROUD

We sleep beneath batik and mosquito net, salty skin
scratching the mattress. Beside me, the guidebook
pages, thin as a bible's, curl up from the dampness.
I dream I'm on a ship as it slides—no,
thrusts—through the neck of a bottle.
The scratchy sails cover us like burial linens.
I have seen fluyt models in museums, but never
the hook: the ∫ used to wrench it up like a tent.
Somewhere under my sleep, the deck is buckling.

I lie next to a woman that I have never met,
our mouths muted by strips of sailcloth.
A scar already divides her bare belly into two.
Here, some missionary—a sailor, a white boy—
guides his knife again, imagines her as a slit.

ALCATRAZ, MARS

They call us *a citadel*
in a blueless bay—

singular, like a snow globe's
stark figurine:

grottoes washed white
as a moon's winter

stomach, something
chiseled out of rib.

What they dreamed up
again, in that old Roman

way: the ruined cake
of the Colosseum

reborn, forever
in the bulwark's grip.

The air here wants
to close us in. O riprap

memory, you are heavy
with salt. I can't breathe

in this birdless bay.
When it comes to cruelty,

they are always wrong—
the old and new

masters, the same keys
cluttering the ring. Hear

the men and women kept
in waxing, separate hives.

On my pillow, I leave
a soap-carved likeness

of my face,
locks of my own

clipped hair. With a fork and spoon
I slit the roof. My leaving

shadow is blue-black, ragged
as the folds of a wing.

Fearing, now,
the swiftness of my body,

the guard in his
crow's nest fires again—

each shot useless, muted
as a feather would be, in this air—

tell him I married a wave,
broke through

each cloud ceiling.
Gasped as I hoped

for heaven's thin:
something blue beyond

this ladder and the gunmetal
smell of his hands.

LOST EXIT INTERVIEW

Can you measure the length of your work and stay?

Not in tea or coffee spoons,
not on wing-pairs turned gold

with August. Not even in *sols,*
those upbreaths of the red baton.

I counted nights. In the sharp
blanks where crickets should've been,

I traced another, blurrier loop:
the old volcano, breathing.

What were your expectations? Do you believe the training you received was adequate?

As angry adolescents, we learned
to remake our insect sounds

by dragging one finger across
the wet rim of a glass.

I wanted, somehow,
to flip this iteration:

regender this world
as something humid, more mirrored.

Describe your home and weekly routine, including any obstacles faced.

Some days it is nothing
but pageantry, the itch of layers

and layers, dust and rock and armor,
our terrain's wrinkled palimpsest. Somewhere

toward the bottom, I
am water, a blue costume.

Was there a single moment when you realized you had lost faith in _____?

I asked, what is it in
this landscape's warp

that hollows my brain
toward speechlessness?

Who or what do you blame for your decisions?

She was surely up to something.
There was something she was.

She was something. She was
surely. She was. She was.

Choose the most accurate description of your current belief system:

"Saturn returns"   "Bellwether"   "Lead singer of nothing" ✓   "Against"

When I am lost, I:

A. Look ahead, try to locate a pilot light
B. Answer cannot be determined

C. Sketch a scene from a Western
D. All of the above ✓

*And choose the **best expression** of your loss at this time:*

| III | Three | 15/5 | 3.00000000000000000 ✓ |

Would you like to make a final dedication (forty characters max, including deep spaces)? If so, you may enter it at this time.

for poor on'ry people

like you and like I . . .

By etching your initials above the horizon: "I hereby acknowledge that there are no tangible exits, endpoints, or clear returns . . ."

★

★

*

THE NORTHERN LIGHTS, AS SEEN FROM MARS

I

Sky is where the racer lives.
Scales blurring from the speed
of light, her tongue's black fork

is lost, dissolved by distance.
But what we thought
they'd driven to extinction

now takes form again:
a neon ouroboros
above the struggling tree line.

Our new ecology
gulps and gulps for air,
but dust has whorled itself

into a pageant we hardly
recognize. Night is full
of quick changes, costumes

tossed aside: blue sequins,
yards of crinoline. Smoke.
Some days, the fabric of space

seems arranged only
for our recognition. The word
beauty holds like a magnet

to my tongue, my mind
a book of matches, waiting
for the strike and spark.

II

Even in the myth, the snake
learns to bury her purse of eggs.
In our human memory, still,

those hills and impossible
blue-green distances
recall an old-world name,

Virginia. It arrives as beads
of sweat and sand between
the teeth and then the moaning

floorboards of ships, sails'
cruel whipping. Whose
father mapped these

degrees, each dell and vale?
As if water and not land,
that terrain, ribbon by ribbon,

was greedily siphoned away,
all the while still breathing
with its Native names.

Whether there were omens
first, no one can know
for sure. We picture, say,

a mosquito swarm
above the coastal plain
like a misshapen constellation,

its gloss increasing
as it drops closer: a funnel,
the terrible humming.

III

The tornado, I read
long ago, was indigenous
to North America,

though what other world
wasn't born inside this
swirling dust. But unlike

the stories of dust devils,
our air is full of hooks
and echoes. Its blindness

turns and turns,
a barber pole forever
stripped of stripes.

In Gale Crater, a flock
of green stones—dry ice
pelting, a noise that holds

both the explicative and mute—
and then an even stranger
air, dropping down its wick.

IV

Farewell, farewell. The snake,
sorry to say, has swallowed itself
in hunger. The night is undone,

exposing its violet bands, a whelk
a tide has just turned over.
Once, an ocean where

we stand, water hushing
this northern hemisphere.
Thinking of humidity, the brain

blooms with lost years,
moving pictures: lily pads
stirring under pink blossoms,

the quiet drama
of willow and oak.
The lizard's lost blue

balance. Perhaps the first
snake, his legs surrendered
in streamlined devotion.

A mile deep, that water
too would have seemed
impossible to lose. Yet

we are, billions later,
almost not able to recall
the old names: algae green,

storm-cloud violet. My grandmother's
mother once looked skyward, standing
on an isle in the north of Scotland.

Bell was her name. Like waves of any
color, the sound of it breaks best
in a medium of crisp, cold dark.

V

Goodnight spade and pick.
Goodnight helmet, bowl,
tablecloth, child's brush.

Goodnight hunter and goat
in the sky, blur and veil:
not enough pixels to see

the ruin's full. Goodnight
old Earth, that far blue
meniscus. Hush.

VI

Tonight, the arid landscape
refuses any human touch.
Below me, bristles of sagebrush

stay hidden, their smell
absorbed by air's chill.
If you touched me also, I might

ring and splinter,
as when a foot falls
on a pond's shallow ice,

my organs like koi, slow
flashes beneath a winter surface.
How anyone survives

one dormant season
and then another—
carrying their bodies

under the weightless winter sky—
I cannot say. The scholar
of solitude opens

the ancient book (pressed
flowers, crumbling leaves)
just as—now! slid across

his moonroof—an aurora
pulses, making the breath
catch inside his throat.

VII

Consider the path
that brought us here—
a chain of narrow, unlit

passages, sorrow
hidden beneath the decks
of ships. Ancestors

believed the sky's
discharge of light
was the dead calling

back to us, showing off
their blubber pots
or playing ball with a walrus head.

Oh, the cruelties
reserved for nights—
war or wonder, the garish

carousel has nothing
left but color,
each horse whirled

out of air and plasma.
There our bodies tilt, tear
away from seasons. In morning,

we'll find the hourglass
gone to pieces, a red ash
landscape filling in the blanks.

Nothing can really be
lost, some say—
not a silver key in a field

of snow, not a planet's
ancient field of magnets.
Looking up, we see

these remnants: ions
that ache against this charge,
a backdrop behind

the unfixed world. Your mother
as she sweeps across
the sky, in shimmering robes.

FUGUE FOR WIND AND PIPES

(I) Numbers, here, like strange balloons

have no choice but to drift

away from the base. The chance of rain

still at zero, our percent sign

isn't doubt against hope,

but simply a drawing, %: two worlds,

or one in a mirror, plus

that unknowable slant between.

In truth, I am against recounting

my own story. I fear wind will split

words back to their meaningless elements,

carbon snapped from oxygen, the tilt torn

away from the seasons. Any sound is found

now kilometers away from its voice.

(II) There is an unknowable slit between

the Mars musician and her hearer:

zone where all noise is

enveloped, a quicksand

composed of empty, careless sparks.

Standing next to the organ, you must have

recognized the tune from a church

on Earth, though the key has slipped some

(I) On earth, where the key slipped

slowly from major to minor,

the once-blue water choked with algae

on the chromatic ladder: the red sound

lowering its flame into yellow.

Now imagine yourself just ten meters

churned hot. Everyone had to learn

not to trust it: the esplanades flooded

while the continents' interiors parched

to a powder. *What now*, leaders asked,

climbing up to snatch the last robin egg

from the nest: they were that hungry,

that desperate to see a blue

they recognized. It seemed the world

was beginning to swallow itself:

the moon's white narcotic

washed down by seas rising and risen.

(I) Our own cells so in need

of water and air, we only have

two slow choices: take a heavy hand

and instruments to the sphere around us,

or else evolve. Does the latter even

come as choice? All of us are Darwin's

away: the same organ, all bravado,

gone silent. Nothing but the hard glare

of pipes, and pedals pumping a shush.

(II) As if someone climbed, snatched the last egg

out of the sky: a suspect moon

vanished just hours after it rose.

Only thin cirrus clouds remain, lost

feathers from a hen. But there are no animals

here, except, of course, ourselves:

wrapped in endless layers of wire and plastic,

our own cells in need of protection.

Strange, seeing that ruin under

the microscope: this one's fine, but this one's

damaged, you hear? The differences so subtle

it's like watching a planet

change shape, when our own lives,

geologically, are just a hitch pin in time.

finches, spangling the sky:

dark notes, capricious in the wind.

I wish I could change. I want to be

a person who needs nothing:

no longing for a calendar, tracing

the year's predictable plot. No heat.

No telephone. No crinkling

of leaves. Not one strain of music.

(II) Capricious wind. Dark notes—she thinks

—crinkling in some vacuum above?

She wakes to find this strange sound

infused in all of her cells, a memory

that must be false. Nothing crinkles

in her life but sheets of cellophane

and garment bags, clutching white coats of mail.

Is it possible to dream of this timbre,

she asks, one I have never heard?

She wants to be more than an uncertain answer:

her pitch so fierce it would strip the felt

from behind each key. She'd be the metal,

the hammers hitting. Just before the ring lowers

out of range: numbers speak in the thin, strange air.

AGNUS DEI: MARS

Less than a light-year
ahead, this atmosphere
swirls and thickens toward equilibrium,

the first conifers
pricking the air, dawn
a blue yonder, the robin's egg.

This world that would not
move, this world that once looked
plain and red as sealing wax

covers its face
with grass, with a noise
like breath blown in a bottle.

Despite the warnings, I'll step out
unhindered by tank or mask,
become too winded

for words or even listening. I'll wander
through white blooms of greasewood,
collapse at the mountain's foot.

Our drifting, they say, is genetic
in nature, a destiny hardwired
in our cells or the stars.

But on Earth—as the story goes—
my kin called out for mercy,
sheep down to skin and bone.

Their planet had grown too warm
without passion.
Everyone had to make a choice.

We live, now, without
animals, don't know how
or what to confess. We know only one prayer:

Make this *sol* a clear, high note,
make the dust devils weaken. Make my cells
repair. Keep me

from ultraviolet arrows.
Let the air I hold be sweet.

Once, in place of the canary,
we sent out a trio of women:
a six-lung test, red flues open.

The younger two crossed
and lived, rushed back to tell
the good news. And the old one,

they call her a miracle.
They say she went out singing.

NOTES

All poem titles with place names on Mars ("Cumberland City," "Amazonis," "Arcadia," and "Columbus"), with the exception of "Alcatraz," are real names, already given by scientists to Martian regions or landforms.

"Red Planet Application": The lines "The brush of another person/ is more gravity than I can stand" are a play on Walt Whitman's "Song of Myself": "To *touch* my *person* to someone else's is about as much as I *can stand*."

"Deep Space Crown": Lines 2 and 3 are riffs on the language and images in Elizabeth Bishop's poem "At the Fishhouses." The first smashed sonnet is also inspired by Linda Bierds's "Time and Space." In the second sonnet, the last line takes its language from Ezekiel 1:16, as well as William Faulkner's *Light in August*: "My, my. A body does get around."

"Backflash: The Pool at the Prosperous Hotel" is inspired by a recreation area in Taigu, Shanxi Province, China, where I lived from 2007–2009. Shanxi Province, notorious for both its air and groundwater pollution, has a very high rate of birth defects.

"Astrobleme": The word *astrobleme* (from the Greek, meaning "star wound") is defined by the *Encyclopaedia Brittanica* as "the remains of an ancient meteorite-impact structure on the Earth's surface, generally in the form of a circular scar of crushed and deformed bedrock." *Sol* refers to a solar day on Mars.

"Backflash: Hinge": Some oysters have the ability to change their biological sex several times throughout their lifespan.

"Ecopoiesis: The Terraforming": The italicized lines come from the song "Home on the Range," as well as the Appalachian Christmas hymn "I Wonder as I Wander."

"Backflash: Seven Catastrophes" is inspired by Lake Toba in Sumatra, Indonesia, the largest volcanic lake in the world, where I spent time in 2008 and 2009. In his memoirs, Marco Polo comments on the Batak people's ritual cannibalism, but there are no reports of him visiting anywhere other the coastal areas of Sumatra. His actual contact with the Batak people seems unlikely.

"Alcatraz, Mars": The final stanzas are inspired by the June 1962 Alcatraz Island Federal Penitentiary escape off the coast of San Francisco, California. The escaped convicts were presumed dead; no bodies were ever recovered.

"Lost Exit Interview": The first three lines are a pun on lines from T. S. Eliot's "The Love Song of J. Alfred Prufrock": "I have measured out my life in coffee spoons."

"The Northern Lights, as Seen from Mars" is a tribute to Wallace Stevens's "The Auroras of Autumn." Auroras are visible from the surface of Mars.

"Fugue for Wind and Pipes": Due to the atmospheric pressure on the surface of Mars, sound does not carry as far as it does on Earth. The thin atmosphere causes all pitches to be of a higher frequency than they would be on Earth.

ACKNOWLEDGMENTS

Poems have appeared in the following publications, some in slightly different versions or under slightly different names:

Blackbird: "Astrobleme"
Boston Review: "Agnus Dei: Mars"
CutBank: "Alcatraz, Mars"; "Lolita's Rover Ballad"
FIELD: "Lost Exit Interview"
Guernica: "Arcadia, Mars"
Hayden's Ferry Review: "Ecopoiesis"
The Journal: "Deep Space Crown," "Backflash: The Pool at the Prosperous Hotel"
Mid-American Review: "Backflash: Hinge"
Missouri Review: "The Frontier"
New Orleans Review: "Amazonis, Mars"; "Cumberland City, Mars"; "Fugue for Wind and Pipes"
Palette Poetry: "Columbus, Mars"
StorySouth: "Girl Myth"; "The Northern Lights, as Seen from Mars"
Terrain.org: "Seven Catastrophes"
Washington Square Review: "Red Planet Application"

"Arcadia, Mars" will also appear in the anthology *Beyond Earth's Edge: The Poetry of Spaceflight* (University of Arizona Press, 2020).

I would like to thank my dream team of editors: Lisa Ampleman for hard work, humor, flexibility, and encouragement; Nicola Mason for her vision, support, and dedication;

Shara Lessley for believing in the book and her keen eye; and Danielle Deulen for helping me find my way to this press in the first place. All of these wonderful women remind me what is still good in the poetry world. Your efforts will not be forgotten.

I remain grateful to the *Kenyon Review* and Kenyon College for the two-year writing fellowship that made the origins of this book possible. I am especially thankful for Janet McAdams, my mentor during the fellowship, who helped me with a number of these poems, and also to Natalie Shapero, who read the first version of the manuscript and continues to be my cheerleader in all things. Thank you to the Ohio Arts Council, which also provided financial support during the time I was writing the book. Thank you, too, to Lynn Powell, who read two versions of the book while on a sailboat in the middle of nowhere and helped me come up with a new version of this manuscript during a trying time.

Finally, I thank my family—both the Rogerses and the Newmans—for their continued support. To Sarah Newman, my wife, who stands by me through the best and worst of it: sharing this life with you is the best and luckiest thing.

And to Lindsey T. Rogers, my mother—who always believed in this book and who taught me to love the Earth in the first place—I am especially grateful. This book is for you.